Playing with She
Book 3

Learn to Read &
Play Rhythm

Playing with Sheet Music is a four-part method for
learning to read and play notated music quickly and reliably.

Playing with Sheet Music Book 1
Learn to Read & Play Notes
Naming notes from sheet music
Playing notes from sheet music
Recognising intervals from sheet music

Playing with Sheet Music Book 2
Learn to Read & Play Scales
Accidentals
Keys and scales with fingering
Playing with both hands

Playing with Sheet Music Book 3
Learn to Read & Play Rhythm
Length of notes and rests
Bars and time signatures
Reading, recognising and playing rhythms

Playing with Sheet Music Book 4
Learn to Read & Play Chords
Basic principles of harmony
Chords and triads
Chord sequences and cadences
Music examples with melody

Elmtree and Waters

© Jacco Lamfers, Iebele Abel
© Elmtree and Waters Publishing

First published in 2023 by Elmtree and Waters Publishing
www.elmwaters.com

ISBN 9789079735341

Music technique, music lessons, music education
BISAC MUS016000 MUSIC / Instruction & Study / Exercises
BISAC MUS023030 MUSIC / Musical Instruments / Piano & Keyboard

Design by Studio Hogeland

LEARN TO READ AND PLAY RHYTHM

In *Playing with Sheet Music Book 1*, you learned to read and play notes. On this page, we list all the notes again. The notes and note names of the white keys are right below the keys. The key with the semicircle is Middle C. The right part of the keyboard is usually played with the right hand and is notated on the top staff. The left part of the keyboard is usually played with the left hand and is notated on the bottom staff.

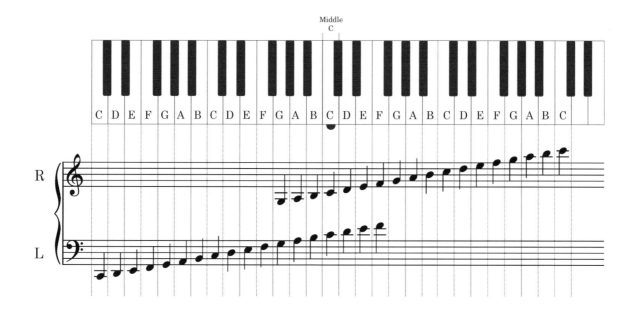

Introductory exercises

Playing with Sheet Music is a reliable and effective method of learning to play music using sheet music. In Book 1, we learned to read and play notes; in Book 2, we learned to play major and minor scales. In this third book, we delve deeper into bars and rhythm. For this, it is useful if you have gone through Book 1, so that you can easily find the notes that we use in this book. It is also useful if you have at least read the introduction and a few scales of Book 2, so that you are familiar with fingering, playing with two hands, and accidentals. As far as playing with two hands is concerned, it is our experience that reading and playing music is not only about understanding what is in the sheet music, but that it sometimes also takes a lot of practice before your hands can play an exercise 'nicely'. Playing with two hands is a lot harder than playing with a single hand. This certainly also applies to rhythm. That is why we have chosen to make all exercises for two hands, so that you become familiar with the coordination of both hands as soon as possible. With each exercise you will therefore always see two staves. As in Books 1 and 2, we use the top staff for the right hand and the lower staff for the left hand. Both staves are held together by a curly bracket. Together they form a music system or line. Notes vertically above or below one another are played at the same time. When a hand does not play, there is a rest sign: ⸝

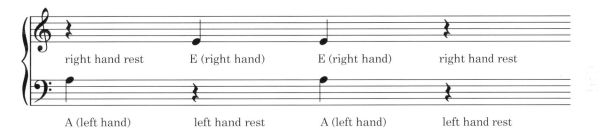

In many exercises in the first chapter, we play the note A with the left index finger and the note E with the right index finger. For clarity, we have coloured it grey on the keyboard below:

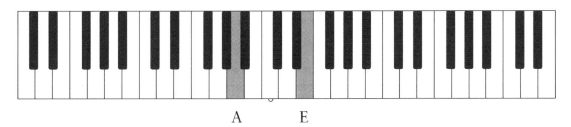

On the previous page, you can see an overview of all the other notes and the corresponding keys on the piano that we use in this book. If you are not yet able to read and play notes, we recommend that you first go through Book 1 (Learn to Read and Play Notes) before you start this book.

Fingering

In Book 2, we discussed fingering extensively. Fingering gives clues as to which fingers you can play notes with best. As well as the notes on the two staves, we therefore see a small number 2 above and below the first note. This number indicates the finger with which you can play the note. For pianists, the thumb is the first finger, the index finger the second finger, the middle finger the third, the ring finger the fourth and the little finger the fifth finger. When, as in the example above, a note has a '2', then you play it with the index finger. Because the notes that follow are the same notes, it goes without saying that you also play these notes with the same finger. That is why there are no fingerings above every note. Now try to play:

We often start each series of exercises with the same notes first. You can also play them with the same fingers. Often we use finger 2, the index finger, for both hands. Gradually, new notes are added, and the fingering also becomes increasingly important. Especially when an exercise is new or difficult, you may tend to play harder. Even then, try to play quietly and not too loudly. Always try to listen to what you're playing, even with seemingly simple exercises. To remind you not to play too loudly, there is a sign at the beginning of the exercises: *p* This sign stands for 'piano', the Italian term for 'careful'. In practice, piano means that you play 'softly'.

The exercises where you have to play more different notes also require more practice and concentration, because in these exercises you not only have to pay attention to the rhythm, but also to the fingering. If you find these exercises too difficult, you can easily skip them at first and try them again later. Remember that all exercises are exercises; you can repeat an exercise as many times as you want, but you don't have to be able to play an exercise perfectly before moving onto the next exercise. Try to literally 'play with sheet music' and you will discover something new in the process.

Pulse

When you think of playing rhythm, you may quickly think of 'playing in time'. In music, however, there is a more fundamental principle that underlies 'metre' and that is the so-called 'pulse'. A pulse is a completely evenly distributed pattern of beats over time, such as the ticking of a clock.

For example, you can write down a pulse as below. We have written a separate line for both hands. Just try playing it. It is important that you play each note for the same amount of time. The block in the middle of a stave is a rest sign. On the first line of music, the right index finger plays and the left hand has a rest; on the second line, the left index finger plays and the right hand has a rest.

If you are not sure whether you're playing a regular rhythm, you can try to play with a ticking clock, for example. You can also use a metronome. That is a handy instrument that taps regularly: you can set its speed. You can easily find and install a metronome as an app on your computer, tablet or phone. You can also buy one as a separate device. Instead of a metronome, it is also a good idea to try to clap along to the regular steps you make during a walk. Another very natural pulse is your heartbeat. Try to feel it and then use this pulse for the exercise above. Another exercise may be to play (or tap) with music that has a clear pulse. Most music has that, especially pop music with a clear beat or groove, which are really just other words for pulse.

Bars / Measures

When you play or tap a pulse, there is a natural tendency to group the pulse into sections. In sheet music, we can indicate this grouping by means of bar lines. In the example below, these are the vertical lines that group the notes into groups of four:

The bar lines group the notes into groups of four. One such group we call a bar. Even though bars group the notes into groups, they do not change the pulse. So you play the notes evenly one after the other. Try to play the notes above as evenly as possible. You do not 'hear' the bar lines in this exercise.

Incidentally, the last bar line is different from the other bar lines. We call this a finish line. The finish line marks the end of a piece of music, or, as in this book, the end of an exercise.

You can group notes into all kinds of groups. Below is an example of groups of three. Play this exercise as regularly as possible too, so that you do not 'hear' any bar lines:

The grouping into bars can really be anything. Groups of different lengths are also possible. Below is an example of alternating groups of 3, 6, 4 and 2 notes:

Beats and Counting

Thus, a bar or measure provides a grouping of notes. Just like grouping the pulse into bars, it is also a natural tendency for people to start counting the pulse.

Below we have written out a number of examples of bars with beats (now for the left hand). Play these exercises and count aloud. Make sure you keep playing and counting regularly. Every beat takes the same amount of time!

Two-beat bars:

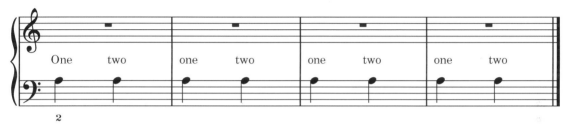

Three-beat bars:

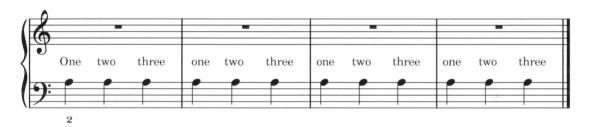

Four-beat bars

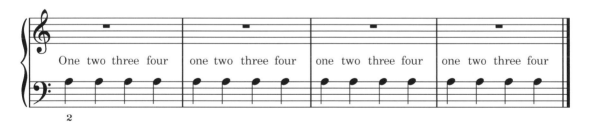

Bars with different beats:

Time signatures and length of notes

The number of beats in the bar determines the time signature. For example, you have bars with two, three, four or six beats. These bars are very common and we are therefore going to practise them a lot. But you can also have bars with five, seven, eight or any other number of beats. Because we would like you to understand less commonly used time signatures, we will also practise bars with 5 beats.

The time signature not only indicates the number of beats in the bar, but also what kind of note we use for the beat. There are different lengths of notes. For example, there is a whole note, a half note, a quarter note (a quarter is one fourth or 1/4), an eighth note, and so on[*]. As you can see, the length of the note is always halved. So, there is also a 16th, a 32nd note and there are even smaller values, which are not often used in practice. The different lengths (which we also call 'note values' or 'duration') are notated in sheet music with different shapes. Below are the most commonly used note values and their lengths in relation to each other:

The lengths of note values can also be formulated as follows:

A whole note (empty note-head without a stem) lasts as long as two half notes.

A half note (empty note-head with stem) lasts as long as two quarter notes.

A quarter note (shaded note-head with stem) lasts as long as two eighth notes.

An eighth note (stem with flag) lasts as long as two sixteenth notes.

As an exercise, try to see if you can understand the following sentences:

'Two half notes fit into a whole note.'
'Two quarter notes fit into a half note.'
'Two eighth notes fit into a quarter note.'
'Two sixteenth notes fit into an eighth note.'
'Four quarter notes fit into a whole note.'

---

* We use the American English terms here. In British English, the terms are different (see Appendix).

In the previous exercises, we have used the quarter note. So, let's use the quarter note as an example in a time signature. Supposing we want a time signature with two beats to the bar, in which the unit of the beat is a quarter note. We call this "two-four time" or 2/4 time: two quarter notes per bar. We write this time signature as a two with a four underneath. The two stands for the number of counts; the four says that the counting unit (beat) is a quarter note. In sheet music, 2/4 time looks like this:

2 There are two beats in the bar

4 The counting unit is a quarter note ♩

Below is an example of four 2/4 bars in which the right index finger plays two quarter notes each bar. Try playing it and counting it out loud:

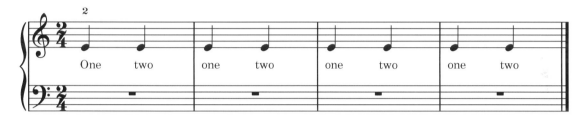

Now suppose we want to play a note lasting the entire length of a 2/4 bar. Well, we can use a half note. A half note lasts as long as two quarter notes. In 2/4 time, a half note therefore 'fills' the whole bar. In the exercise below, you must therefore 'hold' every half note for two beats. Try it while you keep counting out loud:

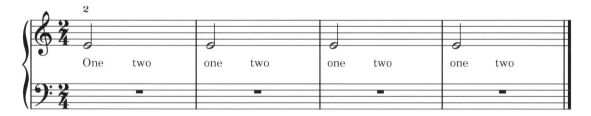

In the next exercise, play one half note per bar with your right index finger, while playing two quarter notes per bar with your left index finger. If you find it too difficult to play with two hands, you can also practise both hands separately first. Make sure you keep counting out loud:

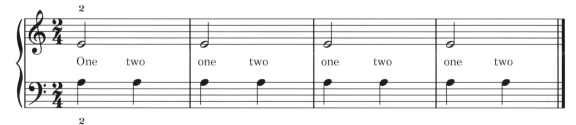

Suppose we want to indicate a time signature with four beats to a bar, in which the unit of counting is the quarter note. Such a time signature is called four-four time or 4/4 time. We indicate this time signature with a four and another four underneath. The top four represents the number of beats in the bar; the bottom four says that the unit representing the beat is a quarter note:

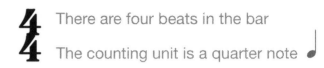

There are four beats in the bar

The counting unit is a quarter note

4/4 time is also written as **C**. This sign has a historical origin. We use $\frac{4}{4}$ here because we think it is important that you learn to understand what the numbers in the time signature mean.

Play the following four bars with the index finger of your right hand and count aloud with each quarter note you play. Each bar has four quarter notes:

In the next exercise, play four quarter notes per bar with the left hand. Count out loud at the same time. With your right hand, play two half notes per bar. Make sure you hold every half note for two beats. If you find it too difficult to play with two hands, you can also practise both hands separately here (this applies to all exercises):

We are now going to practise the whole note. With your right hand, play four quarter notes per bar. Count out loud at the same time. With your left hand, play one whole note per bar. Make sure you hold each whole note for four beats:

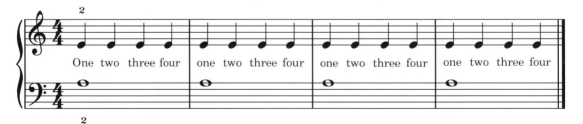

We are now going to look at the 3/4 bar. That is a time signature with three beats per bar, where the counting unit is a quarter note again. We indicate this time signature with a three and a four underneath. The top number represents the three beats in the bar; the bottom four says that the counting unit is a quarter note:

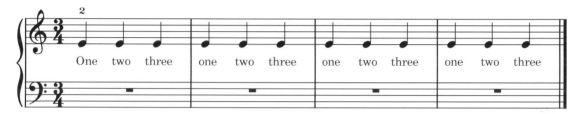

With your right index finger, play the following four bars and count aloud with each quarter note you play (1, 2, 3 / 1, 2, 3, etc.). Each bar has three quarter notes:

In the next exercise, the idea is to play one note per bar lasting three beats. But, in a bar where the quarter note lasts one beat, a half note lasts two beats and a whole note four, how do we write a note that lasts three beats? We do this by writing a dot after the half note. The dot means that a note becomes one and a half times as long. With a half note, a dot adds the duration of a quarter note. So, the duration of a half note with a dot is the same as three quarter notes:

$$\text{\musicnote} = \text{\musicnote} + \text{\musicnote} = \text{\musicnote} + \text{\musicnote} + \text{\musicnote}$$

We also call this note a 'dotted' note. In the sheet music below, the right hand holds the dotted note for three beats:

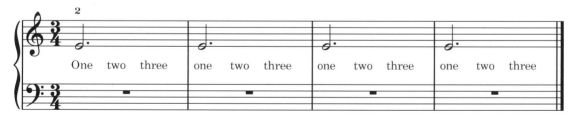

Keep counting 1, 2, 3 while the right plays dotted half notes and the left plays quarter notes:

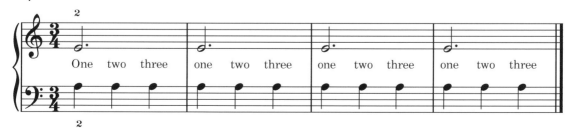

To clearly differentiate between a dotted half note and a 'normal' half note, we can do another exercise in 3/4 time. Now, on the first beat, play a half note (without a dot) with your right hand. This lasts two beats. The last beat in the bar therefore gets a rest. With the left hand, we play two quarter notes for the first two beats of the bar. The left hand therefore also gets a rest on the last beat. So, both hands release the keys on the third beat:

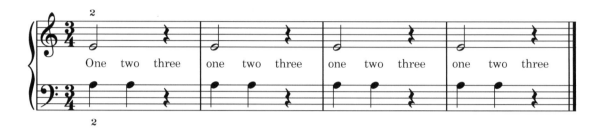

If you look closely at the exercise above, you can see that the rest sign ⌐ has the same duration as a quarter note. We therefore call this rest sign a quarter rest.

So far, we have looked at time signatures where the beat is always a quarter note. But the beat can, of course, also be another note value. For example, let's look at a time signature with six eighth beats. Such a time signature is called 6/8 time. We write this time signature as a six with an eight underneath. The six stands for the number of beats in the bar; the eight says that the beat is represented by an eighth note:

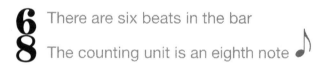

As you can see in the exercise below, the eighths are divided into two groups of three. This is a notation that is characteristic of 6/8 time. Note that we now use eighth notes for one beat, while in the previous time signatures we used quarter notes for one beat. You might tend to play the eighth notes faster than you played the quarter notes, but there's no reason for that. The 6/8 time signature says there are 6 beats in a bar, but says nothing about the speed at which you have to play. Try doing the exercise. Count as quickly as you did in the previous exercises:

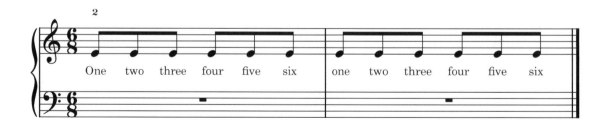

Before you do the next exercise, try to understand what it says. The left plays a dotted half note; this lasts for six beats in 6/8 time.

A half note is as long as two quarter notes and as long as four eighth notes:

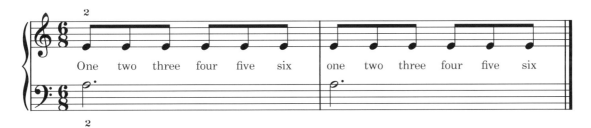

A dotted half note is one and a half times as long. That's as long as three quarter notes and as long as six eighth notes:

So, a dotted half note fills a whole bar in 6/8. Have a go at playing it:

In a similar way, you can also calculate the length of a dotted quarter note:

In the following exercise, play eighth notes with the right hand and dotted quarter notes with the left hand:

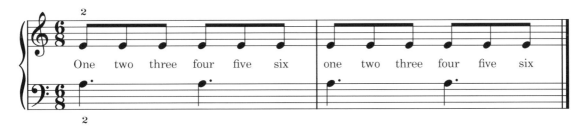

A dotted quarter rest lasts as long as a dotted quarter note:

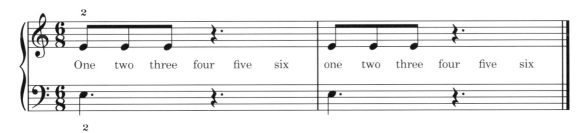

We conclude the introduction to time signatures with a bar with two beats, where the beat is represented by a half note. Such a time signature is called 2/2 time. We write this as a two with a two underneath. The top two represents the number of beats in the bar; the bottom two says that the beat is a half note:

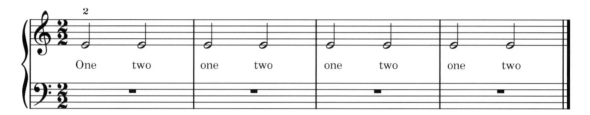

There are two beats in the bar

The counting unit is a half note

In sheet music we write each beat as a half note in this time signature. So, each bar gets two half notes. The 2/2 time signature says there are 2 beats in a bar, but says nothing about the speed at which you have to play. So count these exercises as quickly as you did with the other exercises.

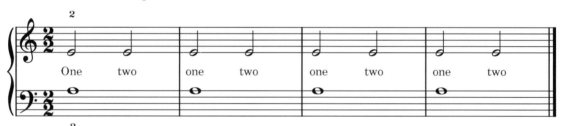

If we want to hold a note for two beats with the left hand, we use the whole note in this time signature:

We have now looked at a number of time signatures. In the following chapters we will practise various time signatures over and over again. Try to remember that the top number in the time signature always indicates the number of beats in the bar. To emphasize this, we use time signatures with increasing numbers of beats per bar as we go along. We do this in half notes, quarter notes and eighth notes. Below is an overview of all the time signatures that we will practise in the following chapters:

	𝅗𝅥	𝅘𝅥	𝅘𝅥𝅮
bars with 2 beats	2/2	2/4	2/8
bars with 3 beats	3/2	3/4	3/8
bars with 4 beats	4/2	4/4	4/8
bars with 5 beats	5/2	5/4	5/8
bars with 6 beats	6/2	6/4	6/8

As you can see, we don't go beyond 6 beats per bar. This is to keep the exercises clear. In practice, there are also time signatures with more beats, but we think that when you learn to play the above time signatures, you will also be able to learn to play all other time signatures. Similarly, you can also have time signatures in which the counting unit is different from a half, quarter, or eighth note. For example, 16th or 32nd notes are sometimes used to represent the beat. There are other complex time signatures that are rarely used, but we limit ourselves to the above time signatures to keep this book clear.

Bars and time signatures

Now that you've seen a number of time signatures, you may be wondering why there are so many different time signatures. Composers can have all kinds of reasons for choosing a certain time signature, but it always has to do with the grouping of the pulse. We speak of bars when there are regular, recurring accents in a pulse. The time signature indicates how this regularity is distributed over the pulse.

The first beat of the bar traditionally has more emphasis than the successive beat(s). You can also say that the first beat gets the accent (the emphasis). The second beat is not emphasized. Try to emphasize the first beat:

one two | **one** two | **one** two ...

When the time signature has three beats, the first beat is emphasized too. The second and third beats are the weaker beats. If you count out loud, you will notice it automatically:

one two three | **one** two three | **one** two three ...

When the time signature has four beats, you can say that it is composed of two groups of two beats. After all, two plus two is four. A bar with four beats has a heavier accent on the first beat than on the third beat. The accent on the third beat is therefore called a secondary accent. Give it a try:

one two **three** four | **one** two **three** four | **one** two **three** four ...

Because in this time signature the third beat is less heavy than the first beat, the pattern is different from a repetition of a time signature with two beats. A time signature is determined not only by the time between the accents, but also by the heaviness of the accents.

A time signature with six beats is traditionally composed of two groups of three beats. You then get a heavy accent on the first beat and a lesser accent on the fourth beat. The pattern is therefore different from two measures of three counts. Give it a try:

one two three **four** five six | **one** two three **four** five six ...

When the time signature has five beats, we call it an irregular time signature. This time signature can be broken down into smaller groups with a different number of beats:

one two three four five
one two three four five

You can also count this time signature with just the accent on the first beat:

one two three four five

There are all kinds of irregular time signatures. Apart from the five-beat time signatures, we don't practise them in this book. But you can easily learn to play these time signatures after you've done the exercises in this book. Such time signatures always have groups with a different number of beats, for example 2-2-3. You then count such a time signature as:

one two three four five six seven

Because the distribution of accents and minor accents over the pulse is different for the different time signatures, they also sound different. It is good to realize that there are no hard-and-fast rules to playing certain accents with certain time signatures. By deviating from the 'rules', the music can become more interesting. Yet it is always the underlying regularity of the beat that 'carries' the music and also ensures that the liveliness – which often has a certain irregularity – becomes clearly audible.

Metre and language

Bars and emphasis (accents) are not only found in music, but also in language, poetry and song lyrics.

When words are sung, it is 'musically logical' that emphasized syllables are sung in an emphasized part of the song line. In the same way, it makes sense to place the words that are emphasized in a sentence in an emphasized part of the bar. For example, the following excerpt makes sense because the two-beat time signature fits the accents on the syllables and words in the sentence:

The following sentence fits 3/4 time better:

Different counting units

We have tried to clearly explain why there are time signatures with different beats. Now let's briefly consider the bottom number in the time signature that indicates the counting unit or note representing the beat. With regard to the number of beats in a bar, the bars in the example below are all the same, all the bars have three beats:

The three bars in this example can be played in exactly the same way. This raises the question of why a composer chooses to use an eighth, quarter or half note as a counting unit. With a few exceptions, there is no clear reason for this. Sometimes there is tradition or custom, sometimes it is personal preference. It is also possible that music becomes easier to read by using high or low note values. After all, different note values at the bottom of the time signature yield very different 'note images'; the music 'looks' different in the three bars above. Yet you play the music the same way! To become familiar with different note images, we therefore practise them all. A common thought is that 3/8 time should be played faster than 3/4 time – and 3/4 faster than 3/2. This doesn't have to be the case. The speed at which you play has to do with the tempo, not the time signature. We will briefly return to tempo at the end of this chapter.

Rests

We have already seen some rests in the exercises. You have often seen the so-called 'whole' rest. This is a rest that indicates that the whole bar has a rest. This rest looks the same for different time signatures:

Below we give an overview of rests with notes of the same length underneath. Here, too, we see the whole rest as a rest that is as long as a whole note.

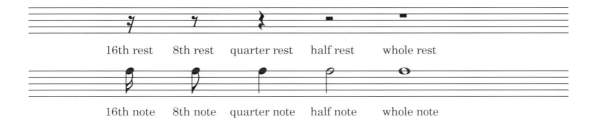

Tied notes

When a note has to sound from one bar to another, "over the bar-line", so to speak, we indicate this by means of tied notes. We use a connecting tie between two of the same notes. In the example below, the whole note in the first bar is tied to a whole note in the second bar. We play this by holding the note for two bars (two times four beats, a total of eight beats). The whole note in the third bar is tied with a half note in the fourth bar. We play this by holding the note over one and a half bars (4 beats plus 2 beats is a total of 6 beats):

Rhythm

Rhythm is different from bars. Bars are the regular arrangement of time and accents in a piece of music. Rhythm is the alternation of long and short notes in a piece of music. In the example below, the first two bars each have a different rhythmic pattern. We have put a thick line and an extra thick line above these two bars. Try to play the notes under these thick lines (the first two bars). Because you're playing an alternation of long and short notes, you are now playing a rhythmic pattern:

Now look at the notes under the two uppermost thin lines. You will notice that the rhythmic pattern of both pieces is the same. What we mean by this is:

- Bar 1 is a rhythmic pattern, which is repeated in bar 3
- Bar 2 is a rhythmic pattern, which is repeated in bar 4
- Bars 1 and 2 together form a new rhythmic pattern
- The rhythmic pattern of bars 1 and 2 is repeated in bars 3 and 4

In practice, the number of conceivable rhythmic patterns is endless. What you learn in this book is reading and playing rhythmic patterns. In addition, it is important that you learn the various time signatures, that you learn to count and that you learn what the note lengths are. In addition, it is important that you experience when a piece of music is repeated. You hardly recognise a rhythm without repetition. Repetition is therefore essential in almost all music.

One aspect of the exercises in this book is learning to read and understand sheet music: this is the intellectual understanding of what it says. Another aspect of the exercises is the physical movement: often you will have to do an exercise a number of times before you get the hang of it. Because rhythm is about the duration of the notes, a hesitation in playing can break the rhythm. 'Physical awareness' of the music is therefore important for a rhythmically correct performance. Even though this is important, try not to overdo the practice of it. You can safely go to the next exercise, even if you can't play an exercise flawlessly yet. Time is your friend! Exercises that you can't yet play flawlessly, you may play effortlessly a few days later. It is surprising, but it is precisely through rest that your playing will become better. This is especially true for the physical aspect: our nervous system learns through repetition and rest. The exercises in this book are based on this. So, play and rest!

Tempo

The tempo indicates the speed of the pulse. 'Slow', 'fast' or 'very fast' are all indications of tempo. A tempo indication can also indicate a certain feeling or atmosphere, such as 'sad' or 'cheerful'. When one wants to indicate the tempo exactly, 'beats per minute' or BPM are often used. These are the number of beats the pulse makes per minute. In the example below, the tempo indication is printed in black. It indicates that 60 quarter notes per minute must be counted (so, one beat per second):

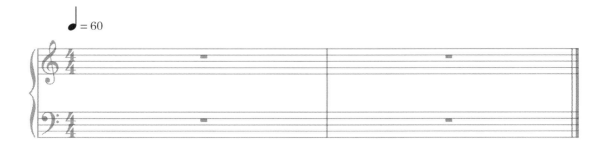

We do not use tempo indications in the exercises. It is the intention that you do the exercises at the pace you like. The best way is to start slowly so that you understand the exercise well and get it 'in the fingers'. Then you can pick up the pace. You certainly do not have to be able to do the exercises very quickly. It is more important that you learn to read and play simultaneously during the exercises. Playing sheet music always requires concentration. When you get tired, it's better to stop for a while. As with all studies, it is better to study regularly and briefly than occasionally for a very long time.

We wish you a lot of fun with the exercises!

Learn to Read and Play Rhythm - Playing with Sheet Music Book 3

Learning to count in time

Two-beat bars

Play and count out loud.

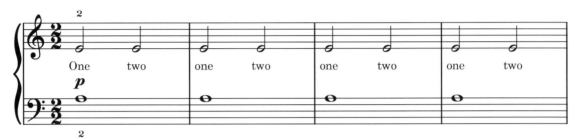

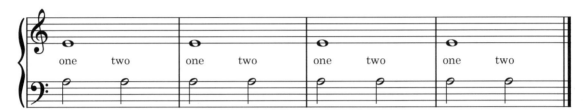

Play and count out loud.

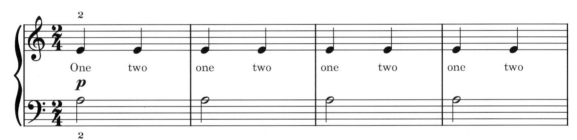

Play and count silently.

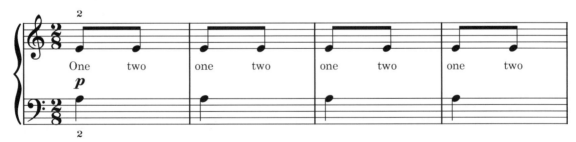

Two-beat bars

2

Count, also with the longer notes.

3

Count, watch the rests.

Two-beat bars

4 Play and count silently.

Two-beat bars

From here the counts are no longer mentioned. Nevertheless, keep counting.

Two-beat bars

6

Count along, note the rests and tied notes.

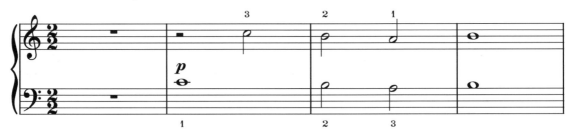

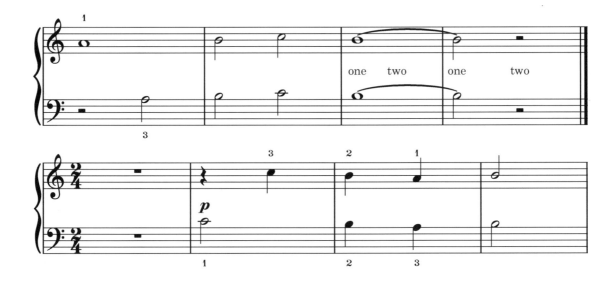

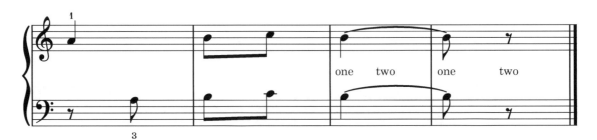

Two-beat bars

7 Keep counting in your mind, silently.

8 Keep counting in your mind, silently.

9 Keep counting in your mind, silently.

Three-beat bars

Play and count out loud.

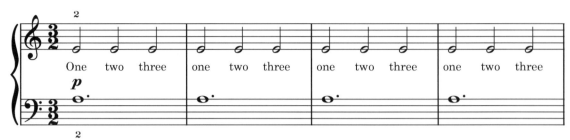

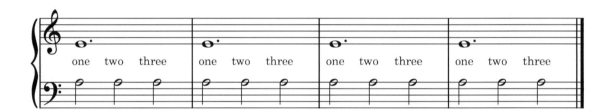

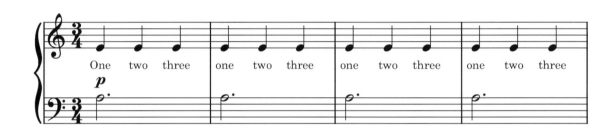

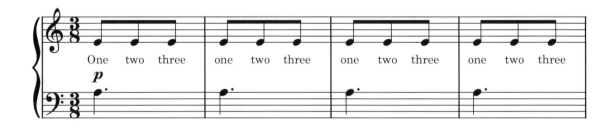

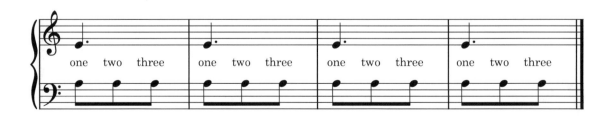

Three-beat bars

2

Play and count out loud.

3

Count, watch the rests.

Three-beat bars

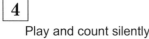

Play and count silently.

Three-beat bars

5

From here the counts are no longer mentioned. Nevertheless, keep counting.

Three-beat bars

6

Count along, note the rests and tied notes.

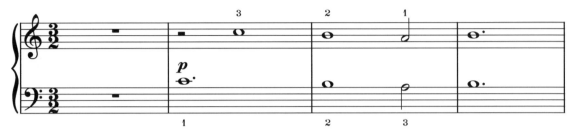

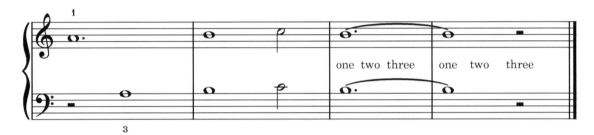

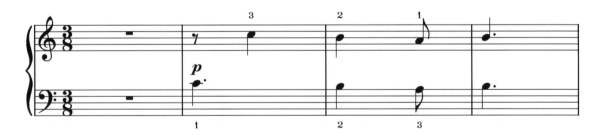

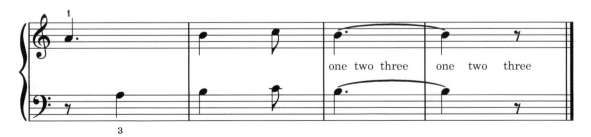

Three-beat bars

Four-beat bars

1

Play and count out loud.

Learn to Read and Play Rhythm - Playing with Sheet Music Book 3

Four-beat bars

Play and count out loud.

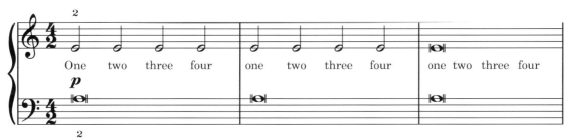

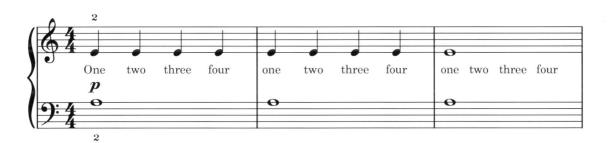

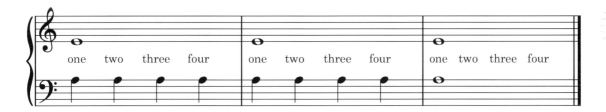

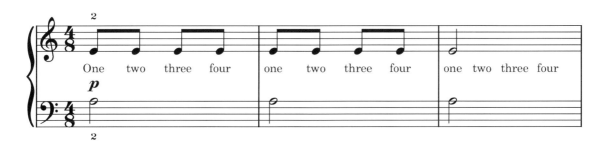

Four-beat bars

3

Count, watch the rests.

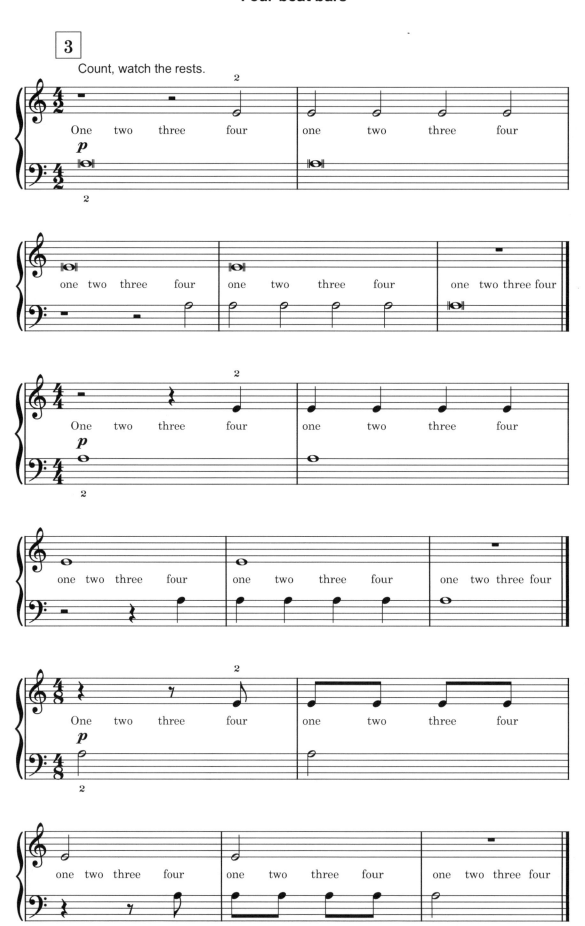

Four-beat bars

4

Play and count silently.

Four-beat bars

5

From here the counts are no longer mentioned. Nevertheless, keep counting.

Learn to Read and Play Rhythm - Playing with Sheet Music Book 3

Four-beat bars

6

Count along, note the rests and tied notes.

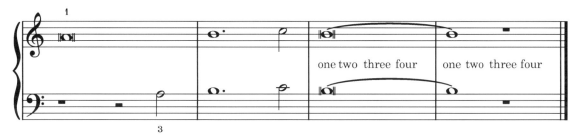

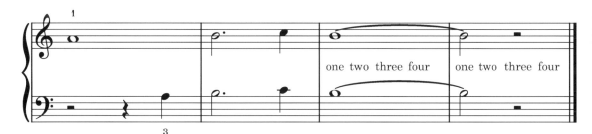

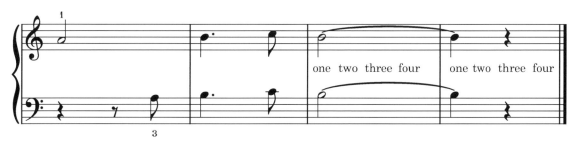

Four-beat bars

Five-beat bars

1

Play and count out loud.

Five-beat bars

2

Play and count out loud.

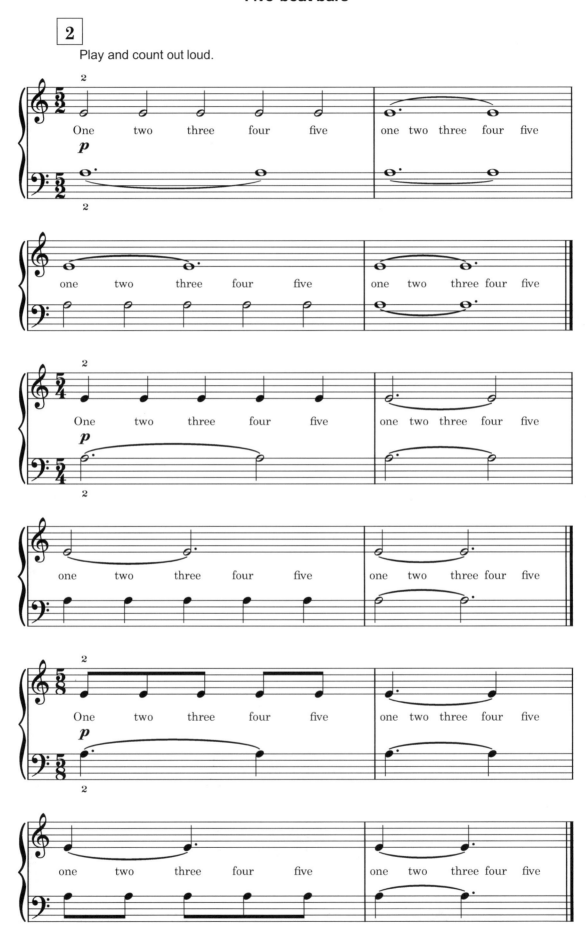

Five-beat bars

3

Count, watch the rests.

Five-beat bars

4

Play and count silently.

Five-beat bars

5

From here the counts are no longer mentioned. Nevertheless, keep counting.

Five-beat bars

6

Count along, note the rests and tied notes.

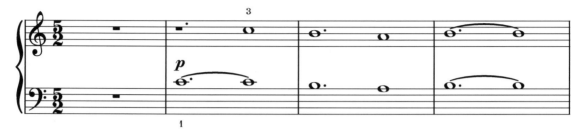

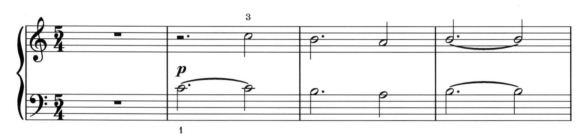

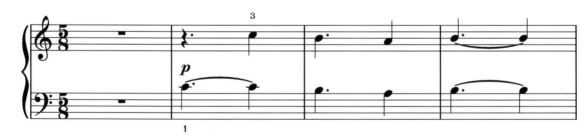

Five-beat bars

7 Keep counting in your mind, silently.

8 Keep counting in your mind, silently.

9 Keep counting in your mind, silently.

Six-beat bars

1

Play and count out loud.

Six-beat bars

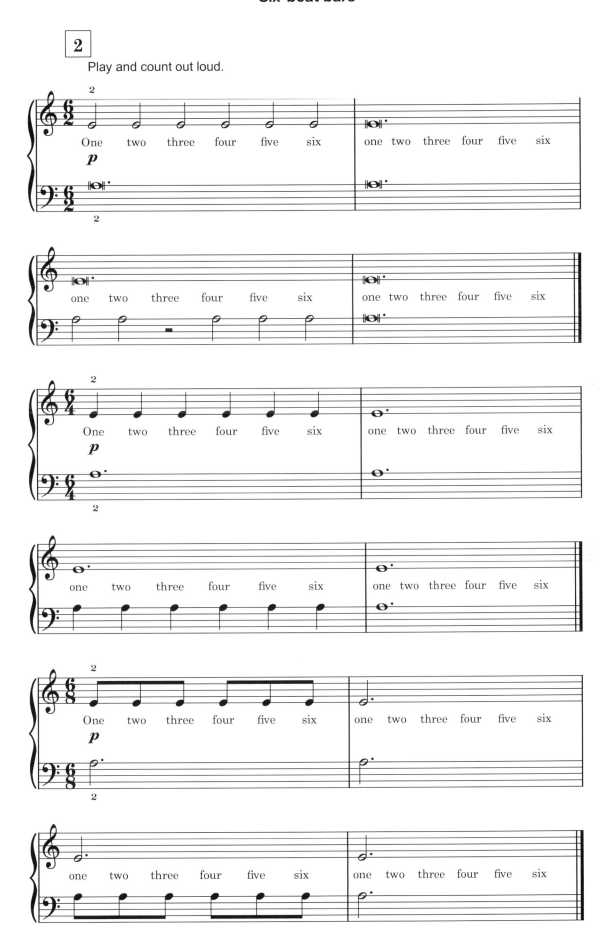

Six-beat bars

3

Count, watch the rests.

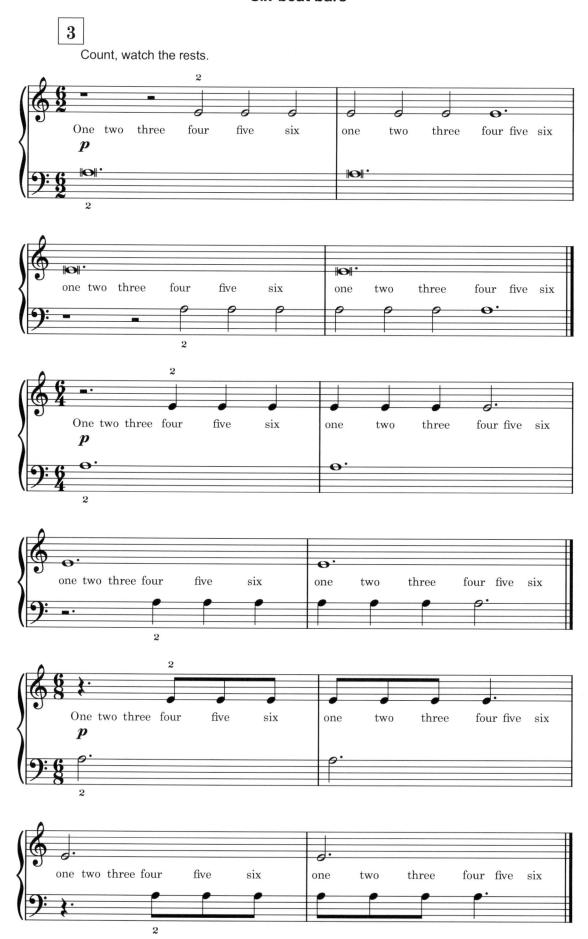

Six-beat bars

Six-beat bars

From here the counts are no longer mentioned. Nevertheless, keep counting.

Six-beat bars

6

Count along, note the rests and tied notes.

Six-beat bars

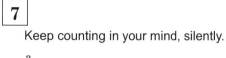

7 Keep counting in your mind, silently.

8 Keep counting in your mind, silently.

9 Keep counting in your mind, silently.

Dividing up the beats

Until now you have practised notes that could always be played on the beat of the bar. In this chapter, we are going to divide the beats into smaller groups. We'll start with the simplest division. This is the division into two parts. When you want to count beats aloud, or in your mind, and divide them in two, it is customary to say 'and' between each beat:

one *and* two *and* three *and* one *and* two *and* three *and* ...

It can help to tap on the beat (on the one, the two and the three) with your foot, while you are saying out loud 'one and two *and* three *and*...'. This way, you stay aware of the beats in the bar.

When we divide the beat into three, we speak of 'triplets'. Triplets occupy a special place in music because dividing into three gives a completely different rhythmic feeling than dividing into two. You can recognise a triplet as a group of three notes with the number 3 above it. When dividing into triplets, it is customary to say 'trip-let' between each beat:

one *trip-let* two *trip-let* three *trip-let* four *trip-let*...

When we divide the count into four, it is customary to say 'and-dee-and' between each beat:

one *and-dee-and* two *and-dee-and*...

The exercises in this chapter will take you step-by-step through dividing beats into twos, threes and fours. Sometimes you will have to figure out what they actually say. This figuring-out is part of reading music; even seasoned musicians will sometimes have to study rhythms they haven't played before. The fact that it takes time to master the exercises certainly does not mean that you 'can't do it'.

Always keep a close eye on the time signature at the beginning of the exercise, so that you know how many counts there are in the bar and which note value represents one beat. Always try to work out how to count during the exercises. Although we are not going to write down how we count an exercise in words (anymore), first find out for yourself how you are going to count. Again, it's easy to get it wrong. When you discover that you have misunderstood an exercise, remember that you have still learned a lot.

Dividing the beat into two

1

Play and count out loud.

Dividing the beat into two

Count and keep dividing the beats (one and, two and, etc), even on the longer notes.

Dividing the beat into two

3

Count and keep dividing the beats (one and, two and, etc), even on the longer notes.

Dividing the beat into two

Count and keep dividing the beats (one and, two and, etc), even on the longer notes.

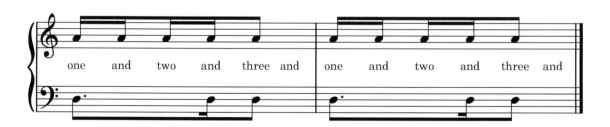

Dividing the beat into two

5

Count and keep dividing the beats (one and, two and, etc), even on the longer notes.

Dividing the beat into two

6

Count and keep dividing the beats (one and, two and, etc), even on the longer notes.

Dividing the beat into two

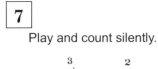

Play and count silently.

Dividing the beat into two

9

Count and keep dividing the beats (one and, two and, etc), even on the longer notes.

10

Keep counting. The division is not written out everywhere.

Dividing the beat into three (triplets)

1

Play and count out loud.

Dividing the beat into three (triplets)

2

Count and keep dividing the beats (one and, two and, etc), even on the longer notes.

Learn to Read and Play Rhythm - Playing with Sheet Music Book 3

Dividing the beat into three (triplets)

3

Count and keep dividing the beats (one and, two and, etc), even on the longer notes.

One   trip - let   two   trip - let   three trip- let

One   trip - let   two   trip - let   three trip- let

One   trip - let   two   trip - let   three trip- let

4

One   trip - let   two   trip - let   three trip- let

One   trip - let   two   trip - let   three trip- let

One   trip - let   two   trip - let   three trip- let

Dividing the beat into three (triplets)

5

Count and keep dividing the beats (one and, two and, etc), even on the longer notes.

Dividing the beat into three (triplets)

7

Play and count silently.

Dividing the beat into four

1

Play and count out loud.

Dividing the beat into four

2

Count and keep dividing the beats (one and, two and, etc), even on the longer notes.

Dividing the beat into four

3

Count and keep dividing the beats (one and, two and, etc), even on the longer notes.

4

Count and keep dividing the beats (one and, two and, etc), even on the longer notes.

Dividing the beat into four

5

Count and keep dividing the beats (one and, two and, etc), even on the longer notes.

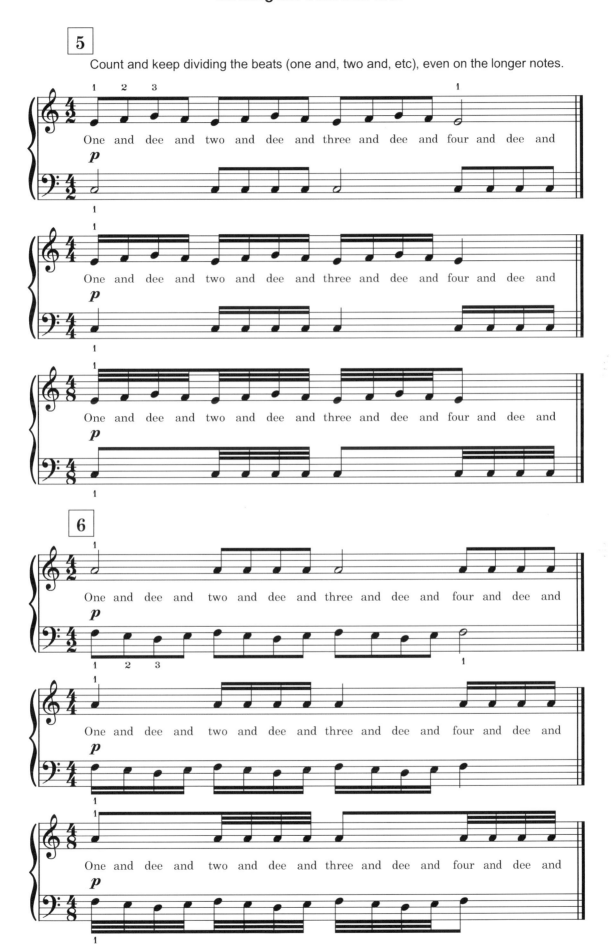

Dividing the beat into four

7

Tel mee: hardop of in gedachten.

One and dee and two and dee and three and dee and four and dee and one

p

8

One and dee and two and dee and three and dee and four and dee and five and dee and six and dee and

p

Combined exercises with repeats

In this last chapter, we are going to repeat everything we have learned so far in combined exercises. At the same time, we will look at various forms of repetition in music. By this we mean that whole pieces of music are replayed. Sometimes that is one or a number of bars, sometimes the whole piece (almost) has to be repeated. Repeats can be seen as a form of rhythm, only, on a larger 'scale' than the rhythm created by notes of different lengths. For example, many songs have a certain rhythm in the use of verse and chorus.

In this chapter you will learn how to use a number of common repeat signs. Repeat signs keep sheet music uncluttered, because the repeated music sections do not have to be written out again. In addition, by using repeat signs, the structure of a piece of music is quickly understood; when you look at the repeats, you quickly get an idea of the shape of a piece of music.

The exercises in this chapter – partly due to the use of repeats – get longer and longer. That is why reading and playing these exercises also require more concentration. Learning to concentrate for longer while playing can be seen as an exercise in itself. Getting to know the exercise and being able to play the exercise from start to finish go hand in hand.

In this chapter we introduce the dynamic sign f. This sign stands for 'forte', the Italian term for 'loud'. However, this does not mean that you have to play very loudly. Piano and forte lie midway between extremely soft and very loud:

extremely soft   *ppp*   *pp*   *p*   *f*   *ff*   *fff*   very loud

Markings that indicate how soft or loud you should play, are called *dynamics markings*.

Repeats from the beginning

The double line with two dots is a repeat mark. It indicates that you have to repeat everything you have played so far from the beginning. When you come to this repeat sign for the second time, you play on. In the example below, you play A A B.

Repeats from the beginning

Repeats of one or more bars

When repeating one or more bars, repeat everything that is between the double lines with dots. The dots are always on the same side as the section that needs to be repeated. In the example below, you play A B B C:

Repeats can occur several times in one piece. In the example below, you play A B B C D D E:

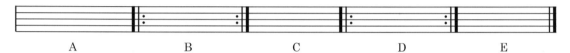

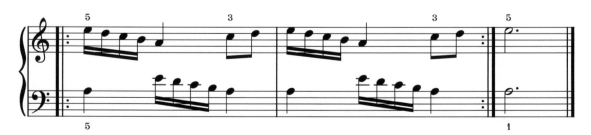

Repeats of one or more bars

Repeats with Prima and Seconda Volta

In repeats with Prima Volta (Italian for 'the first time') and Seconda Volta ('the second time'), the first time around, you play the section under 1. At the repeat sign - this is the second time - you repeat from the beginning, but skip everything that is under 1 and play straight through from 2.

In the example below, you play A B A C:

Repeats with Prima and Seconda Volta

Repeats with Da Capo al Fine

Repeats with Da Capo al Fine (from the 'head to the end') are also abbreviated as D.C. al Fine, or D.C. In this form of repetition, you first play the whole piece, then you repeat from the beginning to Fine.

In the example below, you play A B A:

Usually above the last note under Fine there is also a fermata sign ⌢ .
The fermata sign usually means that you can hold the note a little longer.
But when the fermata sign is used in a repeat, this does not mean that you necessarily have to hold it longer.

Repeats with Da Capo al Fine

2

Please note the accidental: B becomes B-flat!

Repeats with Dal Segno al Fine

When repeating with Dal Segno al Fine ('from the sign to the end'), repeat from the sign 𝄋 and end at Fine.

In the example below, you play A B C B:

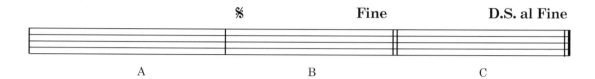

Repeats with Dal Segno al Fine

Repeats with Coda

In repetitions with Da Capo al Coda (from the 'head' to the 'tail'), first time around, you play until 'D.C. al Coda'. Then, you repeat from the beginning to 'al Coda'. After that, you'll go straight to the Coda sign ⊕.

In the example below, you play A B A C:

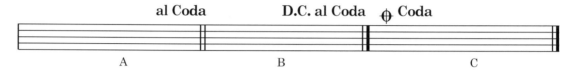

Da Capo al Coda works just like Prima and Seconda Volta, but is mainly used when the repetitions are longer than a few bars.

Repeats with Coda

Made in United States
Troutdale, OR
01/05/2025

27644116R00058